Dinosaur Graveyards in Australia

by Grace Hansen

Abdo
DINOSAUR GRAVEYARDS
Kids

Abdo Kids Jumbo is an Imprint of Abdo Kids
abdobooks.com

abdobooks.com

Published by Abdo Kids, a division of ABDO, P.O. Box 398166, Minneapolis, Minnesota 55439.
Copyright © 2022 by Abdo Consulting Group, Inc. International copyrights reserved in all countries.
No part of this book may be reproduced in any form without written permission from the publisher.
Abdo Kids Jumbo™ is a trademark and logo of Abdo Kids.

Printed in the United States of America, North Mankato, Minnesota.

102021

012022

Photo Credits: Alamy, Getty Images, iStock, Science Source, Shutterstock,
©London looks p16-17 / CC BY 2.0, ©Queensland Museum - Gary Cranitch p17, ©Masato Hattori p21

Production Contributors: Teddy Borth, Jennie Forsberg, Grace Hansen
Design Contributors: Candice Keimig, Pakou Moua

Library of Congress Control Number: 2021940139
Publisher's Cataloging-in-Publication Data

Names: Hansen, Grace, author.

Title: Dinosaur graveyards in Australia / by Grace Hansen

Description: Minneapolis, Minnesota : Abdo Kids, 2022 | Series: Dinosaur graveyards | Includes online
    resources and index.

Identifiers: ISBN 9781098209469 (lib. bdg.) | ISBN 9781098260170 (ebook) | ISBN 9781098260521
    (Read-to-Me ebook)

Subjects: LCSH: Dinosaurs--Juvenile literature. | Fossils--Juvenile literature. | Paleontology--Australia--
    Juvenile literature. | Paleontology--Juvenile literature. | Paleontological excavations--Juvenile literature.

Classification: DDC 567--dc23

Table of Contents

Dinosaurs of Australia

Dinosaurs lived between 245 and 66 million years ago. After a dinosaur's death, its remains could turn to fossil if the conditions were right. This process takes more than 10,000 years!

Every continent has dinosaur fossils, including Australia. Fossils are often found in **rock formations**. Some formations hold more remains than others!

Mackunda Formation

There are many formations in Queensland, Australia. The Mackunda Formation held one of the most famous Australian dinosaurs.

Muttaburrasaurus

Mackunda Formation

Queensland

- Ornithopod
- Early Cretaceous
- Herbivore
- Large, inflatable crest on snout

9

Winton Formation

The Winton Formation holds many unique fossils. Two different dinosaurs were found next to each other. One may have been **preying** on the other.

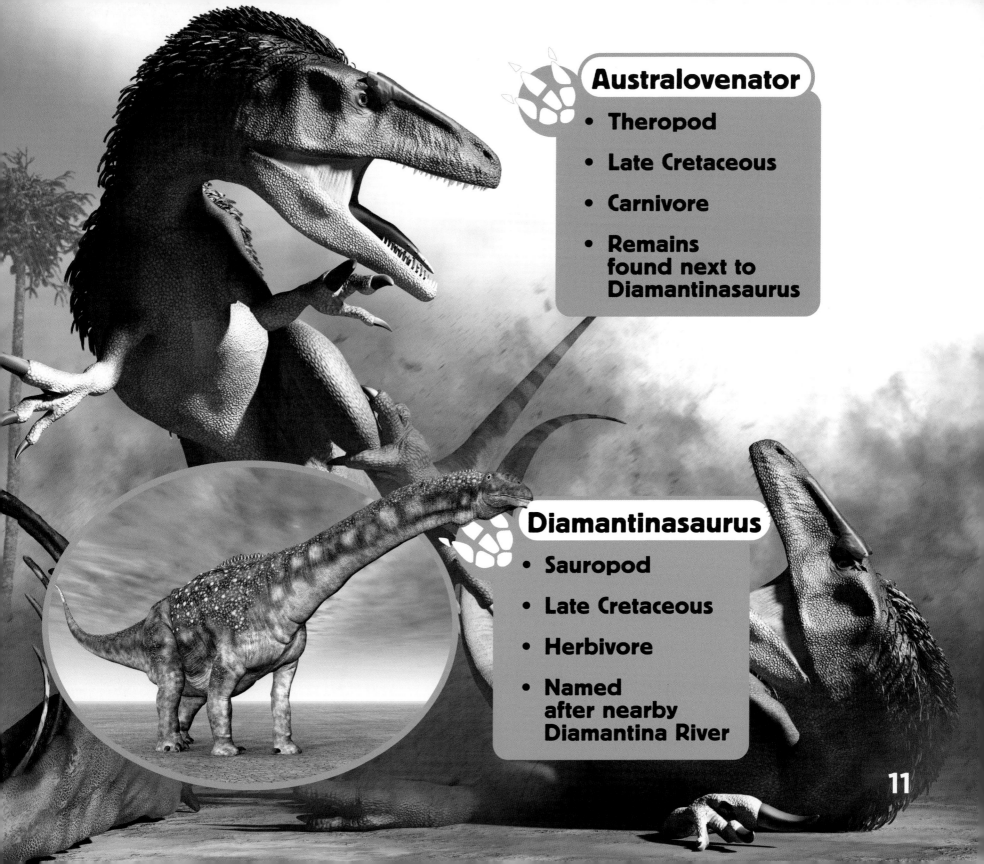

Australovenator

- Theropod
- Late Cretaceous
- Carnivore
- Remains found next to Diamantinasaurus

Diamantinasaurus

- Sauropod
- Late Cretaceous
- Herbivore
- Named after nearby Diamantina River

11

Remains of Australotitan were found in the formation in 2005. It is the largest dinosaur **species** to be discovered in Australia!

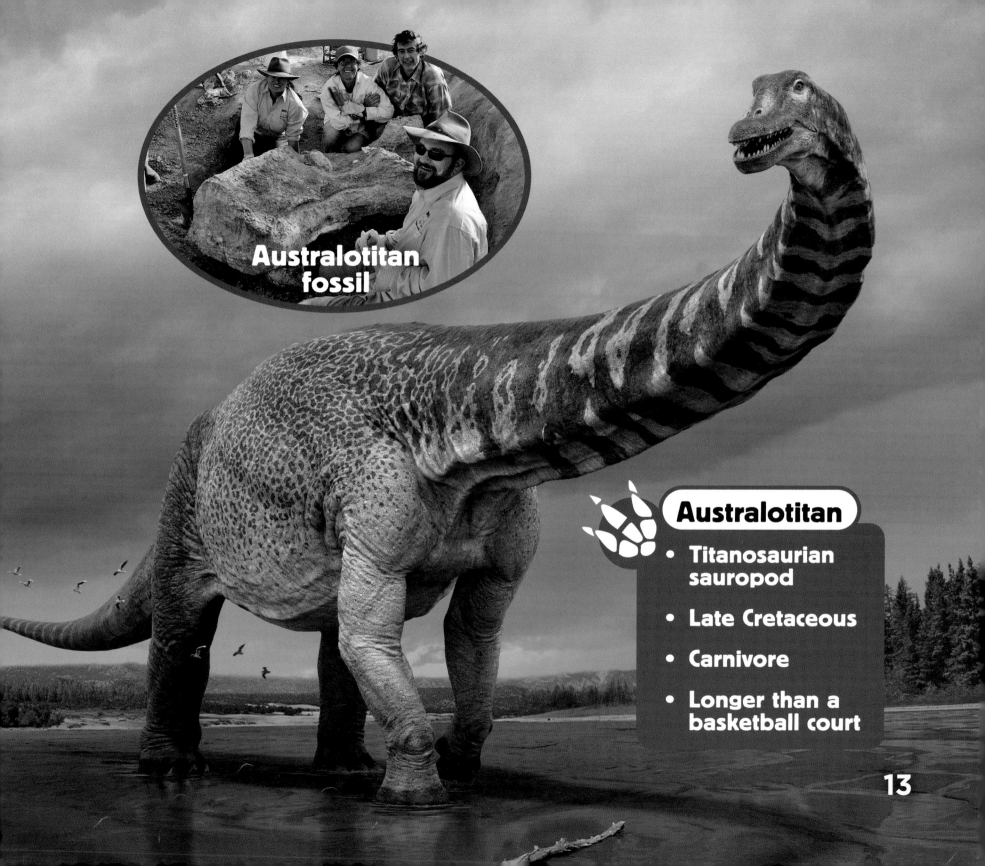

Australotitan fossil

Australotitan

- Titanosaurian sauropod
- Late Cretaceous
- Carnivore
- Longer than a basketball court

13

Toolebuc Formation

Plesiosaur remains have been found in the Toolebuc Formation in Queensland. Plesiosaurs were not dinosaurs. They were swimming **reptiles**.

Toolebuc Formation

Queensland

Kronosaurus

- Plesiosaur
- Early Cretaceous
- Carnivore
- Twice the length of a great white shark

Kronosaurus fossil

15

Bungil Formation

Minmi remains have been found in a few Queensland locations. The first was found in the Bungil Formation.

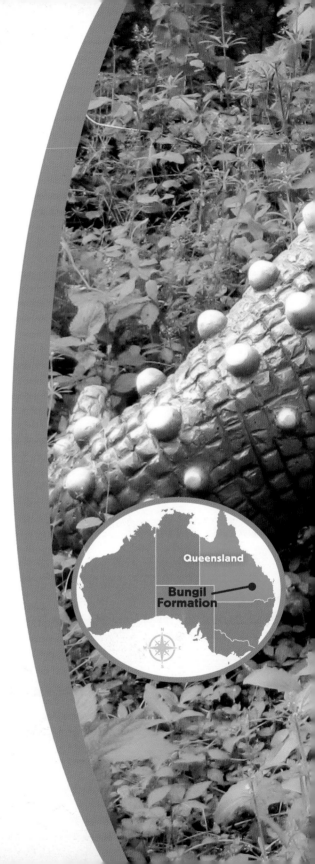

Minmi

- Ankylosaurian
- Early Cretaceous
- Herbivore
- Shorter than a car
- Same weight as a grizzly bear

Minmi fossil

Eumeralla Formation

Dinosaur Cove is in Victoria, Australia. It is part of the Eumeralla Formation. The rock there is very hard. Special equipment must be used to uncover fossils.

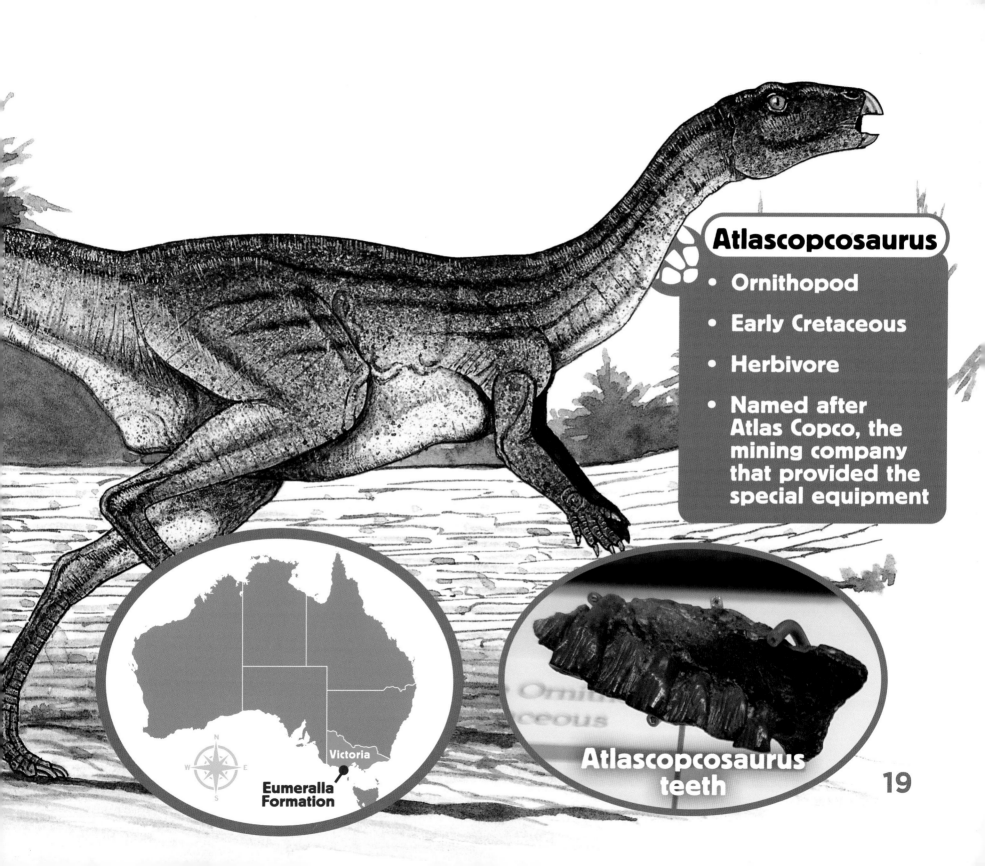

Atlascopcosaurus

- **Ornithopod**
- **Early Cretaceous**
- **Herbivore**
- **Named after Atlas Copco, the mining company that provided the special equipment**

Victoria

Eumeralla Formation

Atlascopcosaurus teeth

19

Many unique **species** have been found at Dinosaur Cove. It's only a matter of time before more are unearthed!

Timimus

- Theropod
- Early Cretaceous
- Carnivore
- One of the largest fossils found in Victoria is a Timimus thighbone

Leaellynasaura

- Ornithopod
- Early Cretaceous
- Herbivore
- Large eyes for seeing at night
- May have had feathers

21

Some Major Dinosaur Groups

Ankylosauria
- Four-legged
- Heavily armored
- Tank-like
- Some members had clubbed tails
- Herbivores

Ceratopsia
- Four-legged
- Solidly built
- Enormous skulls
- Long horns
- Sharp beaks
- Herbivores

Ornithischia

Ornithopoda
- Two-legged
- Beaked
- Had cheek teeth
- Herbivores

Stegosauria
- Four-legged
- Small heads
- Heavy, bony plates with sharp spikes down the backbone
- Herbivores

Sauropoda
- Four-legged
- Very large
- Long necks and tails
- Small heads
- Herbivores

Saurichia

Theropoda
- Two-legged
- From small and delicate to very large in size
- Small arms
- Carnivores and omnivores

Glossary

carnivore – an animal that eats other animals.

herbivore – an animal that feeds only on plants.

omnivore – an animal that eats both plants and other animals.

preying – hunting another animal for food.

reptile – a cold-blooded animal with a skeleton inside its body and dry scales or hard plates on its skin. Some kinds of reptiles live in water, but use their noses to breathe air into their lungs.

rock formation – a large body of rock that has a consistent set of physical characteristics that make it stand out from other bodies of rock nearby.

species – a group of living things that look very much alike and can have young together.

Index

Abdo Kids
ONLINE
FREE! ONLINE MULTIMEDIA RESOURCES

Visit **abdokids.com**
to access crafts, games,
videos, and more!

Use Abdo Kids code
DDK9469
or scan this QR code!

24